YELLOW FLOWER GILLS ME WHOLE

multiverse

Series Editor
Chris Martin

Cover Description

The cover of this book features a silhouetted drawing of a cluster of twenty sulfur tuft mushrooms connected at the root. The mushrooms have red-brown fading to light yellow stems, light yellow gills, and pale yellow caps with a brown center. The mushrooms flare outward, twining together and apart, into the open space of the cover, which is flooded with a shade of yellow lighter than the mushrooms. The title and the author's name appear in a lowercase serif font, with the title set in black, the letters of the word "poems" set in alternating shades of red and brown, and the author's name set in a warm orange-red. The artwork was likely drawn in an art class in the Avon or Severn region of England in 1892.

YELLOW FLOWER GILLS ME WHOLE

Poems

Sid Ghosh

MILKWEED EDITIONS

(800) 520-6455
milkweed.org

Published 2025 by Milkweed Editions
Printed in Canada
Cover design by Mary Austin Speaker
25 26 27 28 29 5 4 3 2 1
First Edition

Library of Congress Cataloging-in-Publication Data

Names: Ghosh, Sid, author.
Title: Yellow flower gills me whole : poems / Sid Ghosh.
Description: First edition. | Minneapolis, Minnesota : Milkweed Editions, 2025. | Series: Multiverse ; 7 | Summary: "A visionary collection of poetry advocating for the excited, the rebellious, and the neuroqueer"--Provided by publisher.
Identifiers: LCCN 2024062331 (print) | LCCN 2024062332 (ebook) | ISBN 9781639551200 (paperback ; acid-free paper) | ISBN 9781639551330 (ebook)
Subjects: LCGFT: Poetry.
Classification: LCC PS3607.H68 Y45 2025 (print) | LCC PS3607.H68 (ebook) | DDC 811/.6--dc23/eng/20250103
LC record available at https://lccn.loc.gov/2024062331
LC ebook record available at https://lccn.loc.gov/2024062332

Milkweed Editions is committed to ecological stewardship. We strive to align our book production practices with this principle, and to reduce the impact of our operations in the environment. We are a member of the Green Press Initiative, a nonprofit coalition of publishers, manufacturers, and authors working to protect the world's endangered forests and conserve natural resources. *Yellow Flower Gills Me Whole* was printed on acid-free 100% postconsumer-waste paper by Friesens Corporation.

For Amma
For Happy Chris
For Baba
For at least 100 poets who supported me

Contents

Tuning Goes Frig 1
I Remember 2
Sidereal 3
Images 4
Showers of Silence 5
Every Poem Is a Bell 6
Giant Rat 7
Moxie 8
Life 9
After the Traveler 10
Rotary Club 11
Tap Dance 12
I No a Poet 13
Story of My Hindered Life 14
Hats May Perish 15
Marigolds Marry Gold 16
Slow Mo 17
Haul of Stars 18
On Teenage 19
Malware 20
Volcanic Mind 21
Hats Have Feelings 22
Other Timeless People 23
Vicious 24
What Is 25
Self-Portrait 26
Greece 27
Mister River 28

Toil 29
Give a Book Bequeath a Mind 30
Meandering Dunes 31
Nomad 32
Gearbox 33
Trap 34
I Am Here 35
I Love You 36
Tin Man 37
NerD 38
Be 39
Infrared 40
If I Cared 41
Nifty 42
Gillings 43
Gearbox 2 44
Demon Hat 45
Ask Me About Where I Am 46
Hammer 47
Interstices 48
Don't Be Mad 49
Aspire 50
Umbrella 51
Be Mum 52
First 53
Warzone 54
Gelly Man 55
Marigold on Marijuana 56
My Hard Philosophy 57
Valentine's Day 58
Half Life 59

Mother Is the Grandfather 60
Xmas I Am Sorry. I Was There Earlier 61
Lumberyard 62
Ebb and Total Flow 63
Gestation 64
Camp Fire 65
Go So Far That Life Stops 66
By the River One Died and the Other Survived 67
Rottation 68
Game of Thorns 69
Bossing 70
Fear Veer 71
My Themes 72
Moonstone 73
Love Stud 74
Hefty Price 75
Hear This Shot 76
Disco 77
Better Words 78
Colonel 79
Mangled Life 80
Leila 81
Mad Men 82
First You 83
Hope 84
Feels Like Home 85
Kelp 86
No Thanks 87
Fey 88
Fox Trot 89
Lie Down 90

Let Them Go 91
Let Me Go 92
When Queer Minds Roar 93
Real Weed 94
Certainly We'll Sew Worlds 95
God 96
When Asked to Define the Word "Queer" 97
Are We Really Free? 98

YELLOW FLOWER GILLS ME WHOLE

Tuning Goes Frig

Resonance is
for people

with frequencies.
I am going

on without
a tuning fork.

My frequencies
go to other

zeniths. My life
is in poetic

pause.

I Remember

Mirrors of memories
so mirage-like in my mind

Mind makes no moments
live past their yore

Some god said "Let his
soul take no hostages"

So I remember nothing

Sidereal

Side of real
nemesis or

savior? I live
with the stars.

Let me be
sidereal.

Images

God has created
kindred fractals.

Man has made
kindred police.

Showers of Silence

My mind
is dry.

My lips
stop and

start on
a clock.

No sound
is real.

You dug
up a well.

Every Poem Is a Bell

I know
when
the pressure
gradient
has equalized

Giant Rat

Finding God
only works

smallest
of the small

or largest
of the big.

Moxie

To an infinite

host

you are still

a ghost.

Life

Leaf falls
I am here.

Ghosts of trees
brothers in loss

I am here.

Life moves on
living through others

I am here.

After the Traveler

Not a boulder
but perhaps

a mountain
that sits on

my mind
fountain.

Rotary Club

Spinning I harness
poetry of the Earth.

The Sufi dances
in me to dare me

to scare your loud
soul to ensnare

my fearful mind to
bare some misery

to bear some truth.

Tap Dance

My fears tone
rippled waters
like gullible fish
tyrannized.

Master of my life
extricate me today.
There is no tomorrow

on sunny days.
I am thy clay.

I No a Poet

Time makes
its revolutions
hat in hand.

Friend amazing
priest pierces
my giant body

into fragments
that I don't have.

Story of My Hindered Life

No stories of
some kindred

joy. Loud I live
lumbering on

at peace. How
intense it is

to go through
rivers of love

with pews of
quiet happy

tolerant moms.

Hats May Perish

Some bequeath poetry.
Some bequeath hats.

Tomes of my sorry hats
can destroy libraries.

Marigolds Marry Gold

Find me a somnam-
bulating orchard.

Have you perhaps
seen a nemesis

of a marigold?
It is gun's gander.

Slow Mo

Love, attraction, and hate are
eternally quiet, manifesting

pouring out of every forlorn
soul. Happening is not

my doing.
Red, orange, green.

Haul of Stars

Give me loud.
Ogle some.
Find me cinders of man
in galaxies lost
to my living solitary

hanging by lone thread.
Suns retreat.
Moons only
circle the drains
of extreme stigma.

This giving of hearts
is best
lest feisty galaxies
haul
the cinders away.

On Teenage

Going rogue is
fiery puddles of sweet
gooey zealous half-

witted Romeos getting
rammed with billion
gaping holes.

Malware

Go go rebel
like a giant

lecture for actors
like neverending

hats for cats
like frogs sitting

on logs of steel
like horrid porridge

force-fed.
Find one thing

and you will
be free.

Volcanic Mind

Hummingfriends torquescrew
language into my mining

mind. Mind secretes
modes of intense

lava. Lava makes
own path. Fire forges

mind. To think mind is hot
is to hammer bones with air.

Hats Have Feelings

Between
the sandy banks
of the river
is the river itself.

Other Timeless People

Others ask
me please
minutes go
into years
minute years
other ears

don't hear
the ticking
of too many
clocks in
the docks of
the infinite it.

Vicious

Hats have
a way of
gnawing
time.

What Is

My ahimsa, my
American ahimsa
is broken. Your British
came to get my soul.

Of everything they
took, my life has
only violence left.
Have that and I

will be nonviolent.

Self-Portrait

I don’t really seek
contentment.

Everybody thinks
I am content.

I am the most discontent
person you saw.

Excitement is my thing.

Greece

My boisterous heavy
body is beautifully
perched on gory

mind. Too haggard to
bear, I am a tear in
the cloth of not.

Mister River

Time is my
intimate messiah.

He lies and ties
truths like hankies

on a torn hanky.

Toil

How the yellow
nasal SOS
imprisons me.

Should you
notice rain,
wear my coat.

Give a Book Bequeath a Mind

Hinges of pages ask me
slow train of my miniscule
vestibule hinges my thoughts
into book hems as I hem and haw.

Meandering Dunes

I am falling among heaps

of intense reality. Pigsty
I am stigmatized childish
hiatus hindered oxygen.

I am too Zen to be forgiven.

Nomad

In every Saturn I see
a devilish Jupiter.

Gearbox

Gaps in boxes
tease among

infinite
maiden
wormholes

Trap

Life hurls a pearl,
infinite attention
to the pearl,
remember the hurl.

I Am Here

Fill the pond,
kill the fish,

gill the mind,
till the nots.

I am here
to fight.

I Love You

between
bonfires
tiaras
astounding
stellar
bursts
dominion
of simian
stowaway
is day
hotter than
gory
night?

It sometimes
is not.

Tin Man

I am in two minds.
I am in two bodies.
I am in some yonder
queer poor ear of tear
in a misery. Tomes
of my mind have
destroyed libraries.

NerD

I belong to the unchiseled

Be

Rivers of I
continue

I am I
am I am

I am so I
must be.

Infrared

I am not smarter
than others. I am
simply privy
to a new road.

If I Cared

I am yoked to beast
of burden, ox. Plowing
in fields of plowed dancing
dahlias, understanding dawns.

I find hassled dandelions tethered
to gills of hope. Man I am free.
I understand. Ox I am.
I forget and plow.

Nifty

I am infinitely communist.
Always be a danger to people
or a miser is behind the world.

Gillings

I can illuminate
I can toast
I can deepswim
on a lost bend.

I can dip my feet
in teeming
sweet biscotti.

Gearbox 2

God is one
mittens have no fingers
simple truths

Demon Hat

Hats are
tedious
venous
instruments
of infinite
misery.

Tomes of
tattered hats
can destroy
yellow suns.

Ask Me About Where I Am

Giant mind betold to compress
into a poem. Don't ask, toggle.
Hand me my remote. A vexed
life to fight big with small today.

Hammer

Rivers of thought I am.
Teach me your current
current. If I ask you, lie
not to the river. Bent truth
goes like roots in search
of the master river's water.
"Hey tree, gnarled your roots
maybe! has it been so long?
since you saw the sea"

Interstices

Bent into childhood
I have tethered
my soul to infinity.

Ether either is
or between
the nots I am.

Don't Be Mad

Energy is transmitted
through every body
beating a rhythm.
Energy exists
in a body
as in a drum.
Ebb and flow is
debating the universe
that is not. Death and life,
well and will, lead and sodium,
certainty and Heisenberg,
electrons and yellow

river.

Aspire

Deities
occupy
entire
libraries
I am?

Umbrella

Developing
a most giant
dangerous
sense of quiet
befuddled peace

Be Mum

Yellow
flower
gills me
whole.

Yellow
carriage
of sun
aster
dahlia
or none.

First

First
I find
mind.

Warzone

I am sure this life
is a dream between lives

Gelly Man

Ballistic missiles
like arguments

man likes
to hear

his voice
in this noise

gels
of poems

bring
the ring

of god.

Marigold on Marijuana

Dancing flowers
I am open

to being
a bee.

Riffing with
the peonies.

Go
on.

My Hard Philosophy

1. Mind carries feelings?

2. God as hat.

3. If nothing were life.

4. Matter is fine.

5. Rivers of beauty.

6. So few of rivers make it to the sea.

7. I am only a flower.

8. I am steel.

9. How life persists in spite of time.

Valentine's Day

Gist of a misty kiss
caffeinated I listen
to rivers of my buzzing

thoughts I hiss
she hers I am
first a child

of the river
and the leaf.
Gilled I sail

I am I am I am.

Half Life

Dents have
mended my mind.

To the undented half-dead
there is no time.

Mother Is the Grandfather

Mirth finds a little
yoked warped
water rock.

Girth becomes filled
zigzag tomes
of water.

Worth a million
centuries
of hurt.

Xmas I Am Sorry. I Was There Earlier

God is here! What has to happen?
I am I am I am. That is. This is.
Half of whole is whole. I am God.
You are God. That's it.

Lumberyard

If my life was listed
gifts of twisted fates

and misted vision
would tilt into place

rimmed glasses
dimmed life

Mt. Hood is elegant
in my back mirror.

Ebb and Total Flow

Each dancer
is Gertrude. Attack.
Not her. The green one.

Gestation

Generosity of deep
rivers deems us
worthy of life.

Again the rivers
find the sea.

Again and again.

Can you tell
the river to let go?

There is nothing
to be found.

Come away now.

Camp Fire

If I attend
fewer I am
more.

Go So Far That Life Stops

Madness
is my inner strength.

Half man total mad.

Tomorrow
is still Tuesday.

To not be mad
is a crime against me.

Have demons
or leave me alone.

By the River One Died and the Other Survived

Man or moss

Rottation

Heal, I mandate you.
Seal the halls of wet prayers.
Leave your gods, feel the earth
spinning like light about quiet
indigo peels of laughter.

Game of Thorns

Again the lotus
reminds the rose

"Remain above the mud."

Again the rose
reminds the lotus

"I have thorns."

Bossing

Another
fervent
Sid. Tales
of what
he did
astound
a yellow
asteroid.
Saxophones
    telephones
        ringtones
        and a tattoo.

Fear Veer

Leaving
queerness
aside
there is no
rearview.

My Themes

Freedom from ivory towers of imagination,
freedom from quotas of yellow dreams,
freedom from velvet wisdom

Moonstone

Homing in on
pickings made possible
with quiet asteroids

becoming silent potholes
is the wasteland
of education.

Love Stud

Sweet person
queer heart
foggy haze

many days
patience still
pays under

the stars
my asteroid
lives rafting

crafting studded
rivers of gold.

Hefty Price

Beyond the life
of the abled

beyond the kix
of the fabled

are the fiery
yellow asteroids.

Feel them
heed the fire

and the blindfolded
can see.

Hear This Shot

Riffing through
ghosts of
tepid memories
illumined by
gentle lights

each light
a rifle of
yellow again
I am bedazzled
because tomorrow

never comes

Disco

Fever
tea
heart

yellow
green
black.

Better Words

Lights find whirlpools.
Can a straight line
make a U-turn?

Landing on
a whim, a word
becomes a song.

Few.

Colonel

I am west of the landing sun

Mangled Life

Demolish
my heroic past
rest

for a second
you belong
to stories

of yoked dreams
and wastewaters
exiting

queer energies
and veering vortex
of stagnant life

Leila

Addled
brains
saddled
hearts
fuddled
minds
screw
the sane

Mad Men

Streams
enter
halls
soaked
wells
in my
personal
hell. Halls
hem and
haw you
saw change
today. I am
escaping
to yesterday.
Can the zebra
come?

First You

Weary words
fear yellow
flowers of all
the raucous
flowers I
choose you
.

Hope

Another day

tearing steeds
off my mind

toward the remnants
of love

Feels Like Home

Hearing the sounds
of dunes of cascading

rivers of lilting words
arouses hawing poet

hiding in undergrowth
tender fire mills beyond

gates of this umbrella
factory.

Kelp

Because roads
go to Georgia
should I go too?

No Thanks

Penises
abound
see you
around

Fey

Feeling voyeur
What is the nonsexual word?
Feeling yoked to light

Fox Trot

Quite beyond
the queer song

lies moor
of tilted mirage

reefs of desert
corals violate laws.

Generations of men
have killed

so I can kiss.

Lie Down

It elongates.
It leaps.
It destroys.
My attention.

Let Them Go

Lest elephants
go stomping
best to close
the gates
of madhouses.

Bistros first
maestros next
lists of children
fists of milling
locusts exit
off this ramp.

Let Me Go

Haystacks, I need
the needle of queer

bees and queen
peace. Let me be

tangible, lest axes
turn my axes. Poor

Mama! Asteroids
at last.

When Queer Minds Roar

Because calm fires
bestow destruction
before light.

Because her diary
began yesterday changing
today and its tributaries.

Because leaves
of my destiny
fall while I try to rise.

Because rivers cause
banks to fail
hailstorms must

give me a rain check.

Real Weed

Yellow flower lover
finds life in the back
of that leaf blower.
Yell now or be over.

Certainly We'll Sew Worlds

May. Be. He. My. Feel. Like. Me.

God

What can be
measured
is never
real

When Asked to Define the Word "Queer"

To be
so free
that it
scares you

Are We Really Free?

Queer poets bequeath
fractionated love under
the lemony astral sea.

Don't you see? After all
seas of seas engulf me.

Sid Ghosh is a levitator of language, meandering through the rivers of Down Syndrome, gilling himself through poetry. He is the author of two chapbooks: *Give a Book* and *Proceedings of the Full Moon Rotary Club*. He lives in Portland, Oregon.

multiverse

Multiverse is a literary series devoted to different ways of languaging. It primarily emerges from the practices and creativity of neurodivergent, autistic, neuroqueer, mad, nonspeaking, and disabled cultures. The desire of Multiverse is to serially surface multiple universes of underheard language that might intersect, resonate, and aggregate toward liberatory futures. In other words, each book in the Multiverse series gestures toward a correspondence—human and more-than-human—that lovingly exceeds what is normal and normative in our society, questioning and augmenting what literary culture is, has been, and can be.

milkweed
EDITIONS

Founded as a nonprofit organization in 1980, Milkweed Editions is an independent publisher. Our mission is to identify, nurture, and publish transformative literature, and build an engaged community around it.

We are based in Bde Óta Othúŋwe (Minneapolis) in Mní Sota Makhóčhe (Minnesota), the traditional homeland of the Dakhóta and Anishinaabe (Ojibwe) people and current home to many thousands of Dakhóta, Ojibwe, and other Indigenous people, including four federally recognized Dakhóta nations and seven federally recognized Ojibwe nations.

We believe all flourishing is mutual, and we envision a future in which all can thrive. Realizing such a vision requires reflection on historical legacies and engagement with current realities. We humbly encourage readers to do the same.

milkweed.org

Milkweed Editions, an independent nonprofit literary publisher, gratefully acknowledges sustaining support from our board of directors, the McKnight Foundation, the National Endowment for the Arts, and many generous contributions from foundations, corporations, and thousands of individuals—our readers. This activity is made possible by the voters of Minnesota through a Minnesota State Arts Board Operating Support grant, thanks to a legislative appropriation from the Arts and Cultural Heritage Fund.

Interior design by Alex Guerra
Typeset in Caslon

Adobe Caslon Pro was created by Carol Twombly for Adobe Systems in 1990. Her design was inspired by the family of typefaces cut by the celebrated engraver William Caslon I, whose family foundry served England with clean, elegant type from the early Enlightenment through the turn of the twentieth century.